Everyday Food

Milk

Joyce Bentley

Chrysalis Education

Distributed in the United States by
Smart Apple Media
2140 Howard Drive West
North Mankato, Minnesota 56003

ISBN 1-59389-216-0

Library of Congress control number: 2004108793

Senior editor: Rasha Elsaeed
Project editor: Debbie Foy
Editorial assistant: Camilla Lloyd
Food consultant: Brenda Alden
Art director: Sarah Goodwin
Illustrator: Molly Sage
Designer: Ben Ruocco, Tall Tree Ltd
Picture researchers: Sarah Stewart-Richardson, Veneta Bullen, Miguel Lamas

Printed in China

10 9 8 7 6 5 4 3 2 1

Words in **bold** can be found in Words to remember on page 30.

Picture Acknowledgements
All reasonable efforts have been made to ensure the reproduction of content has been done with the con-
sent of copyright owners. If you are aware of any unintentional omissions please contact the publishers
directly so that any necessary corrections may be made for future editions.

Anthony Blake Photo Library: Tim Hill 5, Tony Robins 21B, Anthony Blake 23B; Bridgeman Art Library: Louis
Pasteur (1822-95) in his Laboratory, 1885 (oil on canvas), Edelfelt, Albert Gustaf Aristides (1854-1905)/Musee
d'Orsay, Paris, France, Giraudon 7; Chrysalis Image Library: Ray Moller 24T, 24B, 25; Corbis: Ted Horowitz 4,
Bob Rowan 18, George W. Wright 19B, Craig Lovell 22, LWA-Dann Tardif 23T; Cephas: Vince Hart 21T; Frank
Lane Picture Agency: W. Broadhurst 8T, Gerard Lacz 8B, M J Thomas 9, Peter Dean 14, 19T; Getty Images:
Timothy Shonnard 26, Ray McVay 27; Holt Studios: Wayne Hutchinson 10, Nigel Cattlin FC, BC, 1, 11, 12, 13,
15, 16, 17T, 17B, Willem Harinck 20; Werner Forman Archive: 6.

Contents

What is milk?

Milk is a liquid that is made by female **mammals** to feed their young. It contains everything a young mammal needs to grow.

A baby **suckles** milk from its mother's breast for the first months of life.

Children and adults drink milk, too, because it is **nutritious** and tasty.

A dairy cow produces 14,360 pints of milk a year.

Milk contains **nutrients**, which are important for good health and growth.

Back in time

Milk is one of the earliest known food sources. A frieze dating back to 3,000 B.C. shows milk being used as food. The Bible also talks about people drinking milk.

This carving shows an ancient Egyptian man milking a cow.

In 1856, Louis Pasteur invented a **process** called **pasteurization** that killed harmful **bacteria** in milk. Bacteria can make people sick. Today milk is pasteurized to make it safe.

Pasteurization was named after its inventor, Louis Pasteur.

All kinds of milk

There are many different animals that make milk. Cows, goats, sheep, buffalo, yaks, and even camels all make milk for their young.

A newborn calf suckles milk from a cow.

A lamb suckles milk from a sheep.

We drink mainly cow's milk, which comes from a **dairy**. Cows that provide milk are kept on a dairy farm.

Cows and calves

Cows are **ruminants**. They live in fields and eat cereals, grass, cottonseed, and hay. Nutrients in their food are used to make milk.

Even after the calf is **weaned**, the cow still makes milk that we can drink.

The cow makes milk to feed her calf. The calf suckles from the **teats** on the cow's **udder**.

A cow eats up to 220 lbs of grass a day.

A cow makes milk for up to 11 months after giving birth.

The milking parlor

Cows are milked by machines in part of the dairy called the milking parlor. Before milking, the cow's teats must be washed.

Cows are often milked three or four times a day. The milking process does not hurt the cow.

The milking machine has four cups, which fit onto the teats and gently suck the milk out. Milk is pumped into storage tanks to keep it cool.

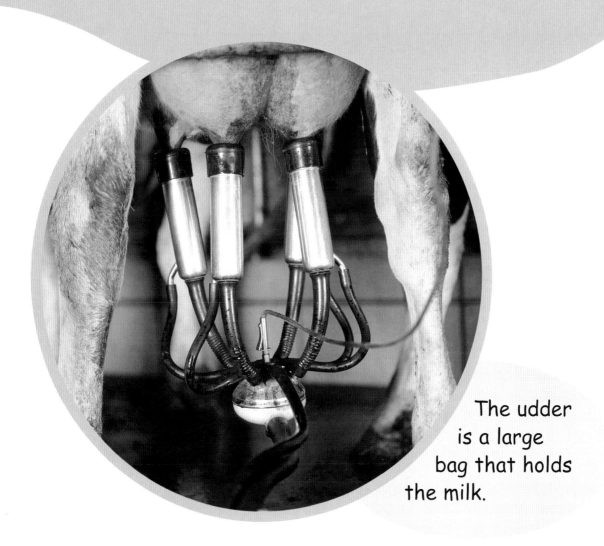

The udder is a large bag that holds the milk.

Storing and checking

Storage tanks keep milk at a temperature of 38°F (3°C). If the milk is too warm, it will turn **sour** before it reaches the stores.

Storage tanks have **thermometers** to insure that milk is kept at the right temperature.

The milk is checked, then pumped in to **refrigerated** trucks, called tankers, and driven to a **processing plant**.

A cow can produce over 52 pints of milk a day.

Tankers are designed to keep milk at the correct temperature.

15

Preparing milk

Milk is treated by pasteurization to remove harmful bacteria. Milk contains cream. When it is **fat free,** or **1%** or **2% reduced fat**, some or all of the cream is removed.

Pasteurized milk is heated to 161°F to kill all bacteria.

If cream is not removed, then it is called whole milk. **Homogenization** is a process that mixes the cream evenly throughout the milk.

Milk is pumped into containers.

Milk is labeled and sealed to keep it fresh.

Getting *to* you

It takes two days for milk to get from the cow to the stores. Trucks take the milk to supermarkets and stores where it is stored in fridges.

Fresh milk is available every day at stores and supermarkets.

Fat free, 1% and 2% reduced fat, and whole milk are sold in different colored containers.

In the U.K., some dairies deliver the milk locally on **milk floats**. They leave the milk on people's doorsteps every morning.

Milkmen also deliver eggs, cheese and other **dairy products**.

Milk is a food!

You can drink fresh milk on its own, but it can also be used to make dairy products. Cheese, cream, butter, and yogurt are all made from milk.

Fresh milk tastes delicious straight from the fridge.

Pancakes are made with milk, eggs, and flour.

Soufflés, quiches, puddings, and pancakes are all made from milk. Cheese and yogurt can be flavored with **herbs**, fruit, and nuts.

Milk is the main ingredient in all these dairy products.

Everyone loves milk

Most countries have cows or other animals that produce milk. Many countries have their own special recipes made with milk from local animals.

This Nepalese woman is milking a yak.

Ice cream is made from milk and cream, with different flavors added.

In Nepal, people make cheese and butter from yak's milk. In Cyprus, they make halloumi cheese from sheep's milk.

Custard, and rice and chocolate pudding, are all made from milk.

A balanced diet

Milk is a complete food and so contains lots of nutrients. It is a rich source of **protein, vitamins,** and **minerals**. We need these as part of a balanced diet.

Other foods that are high in protein are meat, fish, beans, and nuts.

Fruit and vegetables contain **carbohydrates** and provide lots of vitamins and **fiber**.

For a balanced diet, most of the food we eat should come from the groups at the bottom of the chart and less from the top.

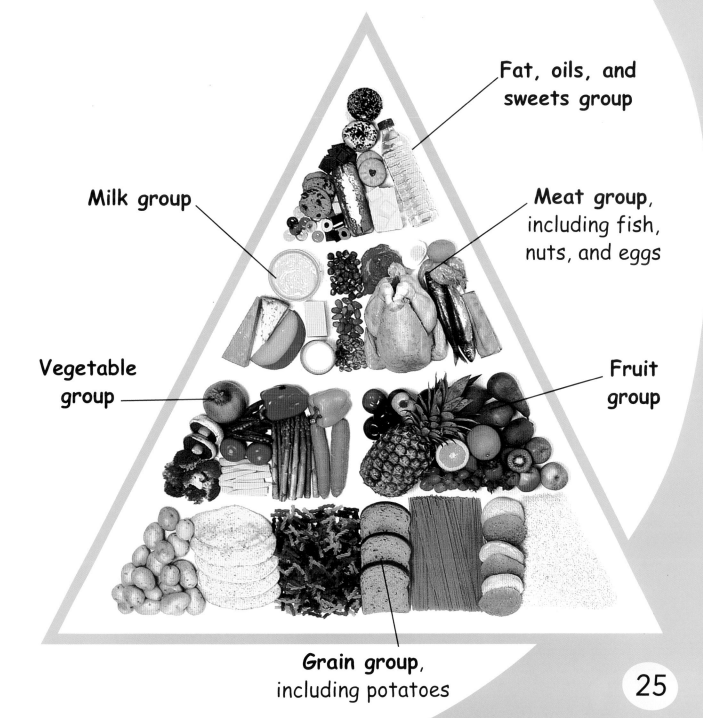

Fat, oils, and sweets group

Milk group

Meat group, including fish, nuts, and eggs

Vegetable group

Fruit group

Grain group, including potatoes

Healthy milk

We need protein for growth and repair.
Protein is especially important for children
since they are growing fast.

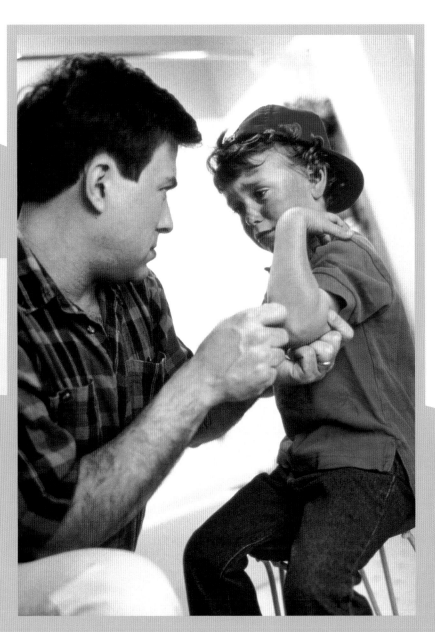

When you fall
and hurt yourself,
protein helps to
heal the wound.

Milk contains the mineral, calcium. It is good for healthy bones, teeth, and muscles. Vitamins A, D, and E in milk are needed for healthy skin and hair and to prevent sickness.

Vitamins help children to grow up strong.

Banana milkshake

This shake is easy to make, delicious,
and really good for you!
Serves 2

Children in
the kitchen must
be supervised at
all times by
an adult.

YOU WILL NEED

- 1 banana
- 1 cup (9 fl oz) milk
- 2 ice cubes
- 1 tablespoon honey
- 2 scoops ice cream

1. Blend all the ingredients in a food processor or blender for one minute until smooth.

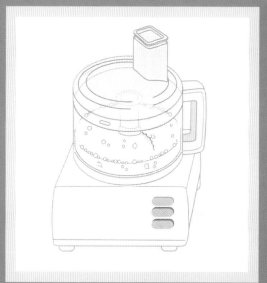

2. Pour the shake into two tall glasses.

3. Add a strawberry to each glass and serve!

Words to remember

bacteria Tiny, living things that we cannot see, but can be harmful to us.

carbohydrates Nutrient the body needs for energy.

dairy A place where dairy products are made.

dairy products Milk and milk products, such as butter and cheese.

fat free Milk that has had all of its cream removed.

fiber Material found in plants and grains that helps digestion.

herbs Plants that are used to flavor food.

homogenization When the cream is evenly spread through the milk.

mammals Animals that feed their young on milk.

minerals Nutrients the body needs for good health and to prevent illness.

nutrients Goodness in food that we need to stay healthy.

nutritious Foods that are healthy and good for you.

pasteurization When milk is heated to a high temperature then cooled quickly to remove harmful bacteria.

process A series of actions that have an end result.

processing plant A place where food is treated and made ready for selling.

protein A nutrient that is needed for growth and repair.

refrigerated To be kept at low temperatures.

ruminants Animals that eat food, bring it back up, and eat it again.

sour When milk is no longer fit to drink because it has gone bad.

suckle To feed from the breast or teat.

teats The parts of the udder that the young suckle to get milk.

thermometer Something that measures temperature.

udder The sack under a cow that holds milk.

vitamins Nutrients the body needs for good health and to prevent illness.

weaned When a baby or young animal no longer needs milk from its mother and it is then encouraged to eat other foods.

1% or 2% reducd fat Milk that has had some of its cream removed.

Index